Double Take

Elena De Ceasare

BookLeaf Publishing

India | USA | UK

Presentation by *BookLeaf Publishing*

Web: www.bookleafpub.com

E-mail: info@bookleafpub.com

ISBN: 9789358312508

First edition 2023

To all of the neurodivergent women that were too good at masking and flew under the radar too long before knowing that there are others who feel the same. I'm sorry the system failed us.

Normalcy

What I wouldn't give to fit in.
I always knew I didn't.
But I couldn't let them know.
Lathered myself in textures I cannot stand.
Nicked myself shredding a layer of skin-
it didn't quite fit.
All in hopes of being normal.

Deep Cut

At times I fear I do not know who I am.
I fear I have become a stranger to myself
and the more I dissect,
the deeper I slice with the scalpel,
the less I truly come to know.
Is there any semblance of Identity left in me;
was it ever there?

Double Take

When you look at me, who do you see?
Do you see yourself in me?
Do you even notice?
Now look again.
Deeper.
Will you see the real me?
Will I let you close enough to take off the mask?
I am not original
and you are not unique.
I am a thief,
stealing fragments from everyone
to be the perfect companion.
Forever a sidekick.
And everyone loves me,
because they love themselves.

So It Goes.

Looking back,
I laugh at how obvious it was
Chewing on gel pencil grips
and refusing to accept hugs.
I never smiled in school pictures
and took everything a little too literally.
Just a kid, they'd say,
So it goes.

Looking back,
I am annoyed at how obvious it was
Daily crying over "nothing"
and inexplicable tummy aches.
I couldn't handle even the smallest change,
and squirmed in nausea when hair was out of
place.
Grow up, they'd say,
So it goes.

Looking back,
I am furious at how obvious it was
feverishly tying my hair in reversible knots
and unable to place my order in a restaurant.
"Stop talking like you're in a movie," Mom
would say,

and I gave too much eye contact upon learning
its expected
She doesn't need a doctor, they'd say,
So it goes.

I needed more support
And perhaps things would be different now
If only someone would've seen the signs
Looking back,
I am livid at how obvious it was.

Till Death

How was I to know that two people
would not always love each other forever.
How can I be meant to hold the gravity
of a full-time job as the postal messenger.
While I am a rodeo clown
standing between two raging bulls.
And I am the doctor,
mending mommy's broken heart
with bandaids and pink bismuth,
the only way I knew how
because thats what worked for me.
And I am a carpenter
holding both sides of a collapsing house,
pulling with all the might I have in me
to keep us together
And I tug
and tug
Until my limbs are torn from my body.
And I could not save us.
Any of us.
I am four.
And I did all that I could to keep us together,
But now I learned that love can never be
enough.

The Mechanic

My check engine light has been on for the past
two months.
My gas tank is bordering on empty.
My front two tires are bald and all four are
begging for air.
The brakes have been worn down, almost to the
rotors.
The engine rattles when I accelerate.
And the air filter allows a faint smell of gasoline
to creep in.
All of this, and the car still drives.
But I have a fair amount of mechanical
knowledge.
I have a jack and stands.
I can change a tire and brakes,
I just have to order them.
I have a fresh air filter,
I just haven't found the time to install it.
I have all the tools I need,
and yet, I still drive the car.

Hues

If I am blue
Could I paint myself yellow
Just to experience the golden joys of happiness?
Or would that turn me green?
Jealous of life's joviality that I cannot feel.
Envious.
Which you already know me to be,
But would that make me more appealing?
If I paint myself green to match your muses,
is that better than sorrow?
If I paint myself purple,
would the royalty of it all be ever so alluring,
illustrious enough to catch your eye?
Make you forget about the midnight shades
that pervade my mind.
Because I am blue,
but I am sometimes red
Ablaze with a fury I suppress,
at times, to no avail.
I turn white with an innocence of regret
pleading for your understanding.
You will not let me forget it.
But paint me the villain enough times,
and I will learn how to style the color.

Womanhood

I never quite felt very much like a woman.
I couldn't pull of the messy bun
or do the french tuck right.
My make-up was always too oily or too dry
and when I let my hair down, it didn't stay like
the other girls'
I was cursed with a stubborn middle part
which only came into fashion within the last
year or so
but I still hold the opinion that the side part is
prettier
despite not being able to do it.
I must've bought my flannels from the wrong
store
because both on and around my waist,
it never looked cute and natural.
My shoulder's looked boxy in tank tops
and my feet looked ridiculous in chunky
sneakers.
I lagged a few years behind on the fashion
trends,
but when I moved away, I learned that my shorts
were too short
compared to the other women.
I struggled making friends

and learned that I was into predominately
male-dominated hobbies.
I know deep down I am a woman,
but I did not feel like the other women.
In fact,
the only time I was assured I was a women
was when I could not shake the gaze of men,
which did not make me popular with the other
women.
And Its exhausting to me,
because I did not ask to look the way I do.
I did not ask to be built in a way that only men
would like.
I do not like it.
Women do not like me because of it.
And I would trade the wondering eyes and
ogling
for anything else that makes me feel secure as a
women.

Eyes in the Dark

I have this morose fantasy
And It's awfully poetic.
I sit in the corner of my closet
Alone in the dark.
Just sit.
Sit and dissociate.
But I never see what's behind my eyes
This is not my perspective
Someone is watching.
I don't know who.
And as they watch,
the walls extend for miles,
but the distance between me and the intruder
never change
But I wont notice.
Confined to the vast blankness of my mind
And yet its all too claustrophobic.
Sleep paralysis
I am awake but I am not alive.
Can you see it?
Can you feel it?

Pluviophile

And on those days where I don't feel anything
I have learned of the feel ways to ground myself
again.
I may not know everything about myself,
but I know I love the rain.
But contrary to popular belief,
I can control the weather.
If I cannot sit on my window sill,
watching droplets splatter on the pane,
I can run the shower.
To some, this may not be enough.
But no one has to know.
As the beads of water reverberate off the
fiberglass tub,
I can sit and bask in the serenity of it all.

Priceless

Meticulously tracing the curves of my body,
he etches the essence of my likeness into his
memory.
I look up, staring into his focused eyes,
His eyes that do not return my glance.
His eyes that are glued to my waist.
Mesmerized.
His eyes which give a look that is not familiar.
Lustful eyes they are not
His eyes, observing an art form that I have never
known
And I have never felt so worthy.

Sonder

I think about death more often than most.
I used to fear that this blackhole inside me
would swallow me,
engulfing me in nothingness.
But I never believed I would actually be so
lucky.
Because I know the shameful truth,
I used to fantasize about the abyss
but I could never bring myself to leave.
There is some spark of hope in me,
and while I know I may never know true bliss
of never feeling empty,
I have learned to live with this weight inside.
This onyx pit within me doesn't need to be the
burden I knew.

Fine Line

Everyone always tells me I have too much on
my plate,
But I have never understood.
I just like to be busy,
I always say.
I function best under pressure, on a schedule.
But it has always been a fine line,
between comfort and chaos.
One wrong step, and the landmines in my mind
explode.
I shut down.
I shut down and eventually recover.
Never learning the lesson.
Until eventually I found solace in silence.
A quiet mind with room for error,
and the racing thoughts of anxiety ceased.
They still tell me I do too much,
but I now have the time to breathe.

Mother

Dear Mother,
I am sorry that you mother could not love you in the way you deserved. I am sorry you had to love me in the only way you knew how. Here, but never there. I am sorry that women didn't like you, and only men wanted to be around you. The sisterhood failed you. We all did. So I forgive you for failing me. How were you to know any better. And while I still do not know better, I will continue to slowly put an end to this cycle of "not enoughs." And one day, when I am a mother, I may fail too. But together, you will show me how to fail less. And one day, the women in our family will feel loved without question.

Amelioration

I was a kid with a proclivity for math
and a fear of stickers.
A love of bubble wrap
and a hatred of wearing layers.
I wasn't very artistically inclined,
but give me a pen and paper,
I could draw the map of my favorite video game
entirely from memory.
I am still that kid.
Maybe a couple inches taller,
With tactful gaps in my memory
blocking out things I do not wish to remember,
but she is still there.
And I can't quite as confidently draw the map
anymore,
but I still revisit the game every year,
and know the names of most of the NPCs.
And I make it my mission,
her mission,
to let everyone know.
She would've wanted it.

Year by Year

At 20, I thought I knew everything.
By 21, I realized how much of a fool I was at 20.
At 22, I learned there was so much more to me
than I knew before.
I had finally spent a year alone.
Learning myself.
Realizing I did love something other than
another person.
I love stepping on leaves
and counting the steps I take in each square on
the sidewalk.
2-3 is the optimal number, depending on size.
I love a brisk walk when the rain is sprinkling
and the adhesive blob that holds a new credit
card to the letter.
And I can't explain what makes this so special,
All I do know is that growing old
doesn't mean losing yourself.
I will always hold onto my childlike glee.
At 23, I am still growing up
and there is so much more to discover,
but year by year,
day by day,
I am learning exactly what I love about myself.

Eye Spy

With all the hatred I have for my body
at least my Google obsession allows me to
research fixes.
"How to lose weight if you're constantly in a
calorie deficit"
Ineffective, just have better genetics.
"How to get rid of acne scars"
Set aside $2500 for laser resurfacing.
"how to fix intermittent strabismus"
(thats a wonky eye, for those who may not
know)
See an optometrist, thankfully covered by
insurance.

I could spend hours and hours
searching every blog
every article
every illegitimate source on the web
but never spend more than 10 minutes looking in
the mirror
loving myself
accepting what I cannot change
and what I should not change
But if working out,
and spending my savings

and going to a couple doctors
will change anything,
I just hope I am happy.

Call of the Void

If I have nothing,
at least this is a life of uncertainty ahead.
An insurmountable heap of existential dread
and a possibility of joy.
I've never been much of an optimist,
but there's beauty in the void of the unknown.
And maybe the future is worse,
but only a fool would deny themselves a chance
to see.

Afterward

Well, if you made it this far, I can only assume
that you read all 18 poems. Maybe not, and that's
fine. Hopefully at least some were fine. I know
I'm still a beginner at this sort of thing, but I
never really expect anyone to read this anyways.
So, if you're still along for the ride, I would love
to tell you about some of the little details I
included. For starters, the title: Double Take.
Why? Well, knowing this would be my second
poetry book, I couldn't miss the opportunity to
take advantage of that. I mean, you can only
write your second book once, right? So then it
was decided... not exactly. It was between
Double Take and Take Two. Now, this is the part
where I should mention that I am a film student
in college. So between the two, Take Two
reminded me too much of a slate or
clapperboard. And while this would make a cute
cover, I couldn't imagine writing between 18-21
poems about film. Well maybe I could've used
different films as inspiration... oh well. So there
you have it, Double Take it was. Now, as I
assume you read on the back, I have borderline
personality disorder. I can now proudly say I am
in remission, something I never would've

thought possible without the help of my amazing therapist- Shout out Mark! But after years of battling a seriously debilitating mental health issue, I am finally at a place where I can confidently reflect. These poems don't even scratch the surface of some of the feelings I have experienced during my struggle with BPD, but I have another project in the mix, if you're willing to read another one of my projects. And I may be biased, but I'm pretty confident the next one will actually be ten times better. Anyways, one of the things that had fascinated me in the past year was the link between neurodivergence and BPD. Often times, they can either be misdiagnosed for one another, or undiagnosed conditions such as female autism can lead to the development of BPD. And I could ramble on and on about why this is something I am deeply passionate about, but I am not a mental health professional, so I encourage you all to do your own research. Back to the title. Upon deciding on the title, I thought it the perfect opportunity to address the identity issues that come with BPD and neurodivergence. I actually split up the poems evenly. The first 9 are the more negative feelings associated with the conditions, and then like a mirror, they correspond to the more optimistic take on the other half. So 9 and 10 are linked. 8 and 11, and so on. They may not be exact, and some might be more obvious than others, but if you're willing to reread this short book, I encourage you to try reading the pairs together and see if it sheds a new light to the duality in some of the mindsets of BPD. Again, its not perfect, but this is only my second (basically self-published) work. This is already considerably long, so, if you're still here reading, I will leave you with three final easter eggs. One, I wrote Hues in my mobile notes app. It was originally titles Colorsh!t because I really couldn't decide on a title. It actually took me hours to decide and I almost didn't include it altogether as I thought it might be too cheesy and I hated all the ideas I came up with. But life is short, and I liked the final line. Who cares if its dumb, because I liked it, and this is for me. Two: While I am a diehard Swiftie, So It Goes has nothing to do with blondie (except being one of the songs currently on repeat on my playlist). In reality, I always struggled reading and just thought I wasn't good at it and didn't like it. A little over a year ago my ex and I went to a bookstore and I picked up "Slaughterhouse-five." After months of reading on and off, it was the first book post-high school that I had finished. Then I couldn't stop reading, so it goes. Now finally, the next book will be a collection of break-up poems. I know, I know. I

can already hear people saying that's been done
a million times over, but this is very personal for
me. And I wrote a few during this one, and
they're honestly so much better. If you have
BPD, you may notice the absence of heartbreak
poems in this book. BPD symptoms can be
exacerbated while in a relationship, but I didn't
want them to take the focus here. So, If you'll be
patient, they're coming. Well, that concluded my
afterward. I would say the new Elena De
Ceasare book "now with fewer typos," but I
honestly don't have an editor, nor the time to
comb through everything perfectly. It's just 21
days after all. Anyways, Thank you for reading,
and I hope you enjoyed your short read!

www.ingramcontent.com/pod-product-compliance
Lightning Source LLC
Chambersburg PA
CBHW071246140726
47996CB00007B/2776